50 YEARS OF THE EFA

*Commemorating Fifty Years
Supporting Professional Editorial Freelancers*

EDITED BY
ROBIN MARTIN AND DENISE LARRABEE

THE-EFA.ORG

Copyright © 2020 The Editorial Freelancers Association with the exceptions of Chapters 3, 4, 5, and 6, where copyright belongs to the individual authors indicated in the byline, and permission has been granted for their use.
Cover and design © 2020 Editorial Freelancers Association
New York, NY

All rights reserved.
No part of this publication may be reproduced, distributed, or transmitted in any form or by any means, including, but not limited to, photocopying, recording, or other electronic or mechanical methods, without the prior written permission of the publisher, except in the case of brief quotations embodied in critical reviews and certain other noncommercial uses permitted by copyright law. For permission requests, write to the publisher at "Attention: Publications Chairperson" at the address below.

266 West 37th St. 20th Floor
New York, NY 10018
office@the-efa.org

ISBN Paperback: 978-1-880-407-46-2
ebook: 978-1-880-407-47-9

Published in the United States of America by the Editorial Freelancers Association.
Subject Categories: **BUSINESS & ECONOMICS** / Corporate & Business History | **LANGUAGE ARTS & DISCIPLINES** / Publishers & Publishing Industry

Legal Disclaimer: While the publisher and author have made every attempt to verify that the information provided in this book is correct and up-to-date, the publisher and author assume no responsibility for any error, inaccuracy, or omission.

Neither the publisher nor author shall be liable for damages arising therefrom. This book is not intended for use as a source of legal or financial advice. Running a business involves complex legal and financial issues. You should always retain competent legal and financial professionals to provide guidance.

EFA Publications Director: Robin Martin
Editors: Robin Martin and Denise Larrabee
New content written by Robin Martin and Denise Larrabee, except where otherwise indicated
Copyeditor: Jared Carew
Proofreader: Patricia Collins
Book Designer: Kevin Callahan | BNGO Books
Cover Designer: Ann Marie Manca

Contents

Introduction	1
Editiorial Freelancers Association Timeline	5
1. What Is the EFA?	7
2. EFA Employees	11
3. The Very Early Years, by Elliot Linzer	17
4. Volunteers Made It Happen: 1976–1995, by Martin Kohl	23
5. How We Began, by J. Trumbull Rogers	27
6. Parting Thoughts from a Long-Time Co-Exec, by J.P. Partland	31
7. Creating a Community	35
About the Editorial Freelancers Association (EFA)	58

BOARD OF GOVERNORS 2019-2020

CO-EXECUTIVES
Christina M. Frey
and William Keenan Jr.

SECRETARY Joy Drohan

TREASURER Marcina Zaccaria

CHAPTER DEVELOPMENT CHAIRPERSON Akiko Yamagata

DIVERSITY INITIATIVE CHAIRPERSON
Sangeeta Mehta

EDUCATION CHAIRPERSON
Jennifer Lawler

EVENTS CHAIRPERSON
Molly McCowan

JOB LIST CHAIRPERSON
Sheila Buff

NEWSLETTER CHAIRPERSON
Ruth E. Thaler-Carter

MEMBERSHIP CHAIRPERSON
Michael Coffino

PUBLICATIONS CHAIRPERSON
Robin Martin

SOCIAL MEDIA CHAIRPERSON
Ruth Mullen

WEBSITE CHAIRPERSON
Karen Wallace

MEMBERS AT LARGE
Amy Delcambre
Ann Hanson
Dawn Husted
Denise Larrabee
Kelly Johnson
Tara Kovach

2020-2021

CO-EXECUTIVES
William Keenan Jr.
and Christina M. Frey

SECRETARY Joy Drohan

TREASURER Marcina Zaccaria

CHAPTER DEVELOPMENT CHAIRPERSON Akiko Yamagata

DIVERSITY INITIATIVE CHAIRPERSON
Sangeeta Mehta

EDUCATION CHAIRPERSON
Molly McCowan

EVENTS CHAIRPERSON
Molly McCowan

JOB LIST CHAIRPERSON Sheila Buff

NEWSLETTER CHAIRPERSON
Ruth E. Thaler-Carter

MEMBERSHIP CHAIRPERSON
Michael Coffino

PUBLICATIONS CHAIRPERSON
Robin Martin

SOCIAL MEDIA CHAIRPERSON
Ruth Mullen

WEBSITE CHAIRPERSON
Karen Wallace

MEMBERS AT LARGE
Adrienne Moch
Amy Spungen
David Stacks
Denise Larrabee
Heather Pendley
Nanette Day
Tara Kovach

Introduction

The year 2020 will be remembered for the worldwide COVID-19 pandemic that affected everyone, with losses of life, illness, sacrifice, fear, fiscal uncertainty, and stress at home and at work, which moved home for many people worldwide. In this area, editorial freelancers had an unanticipated advantage, since most of us are accustomed to working from home (#wfh). Nevertheless, the pandemic still left many freelancers vulnerable to the economic slowdown and other unknowns. Throughout this challenging time, the Editorial Freelancers Association (EFA) remained an active organization, continuing our work in service to our members and also the many people who saw this shutdown as an opportunity to launch their freelance careers.

This longtime tradition of support is a big part of what our organization celebrates as we mark a milestone for the organization: The EFA's fiftieth anniversary.

The EFA looks very different today than it did ten years ago, and even more so than twenty-five years ago, when we last published a booklet commemorating an anniversary of the group. As we look back, we can see how the EFA has reflected the changing world. For example, as new technologies develop, the EFA makes use of them to better communicate with and support our members. Not everything at the EFA changes as quickly as the world around us, as this group of busy freelancers—all volunteers in our roles with the EFA—can attest, but our movement with the times is remarkable. As the world goes, so goes the EFA! And we continue to move forward in ways that best support our growing membership.

ROBIN MARTIN AND DENISE LARRABEE

Some of the things we were looking forward to as 2020 began were necessarily sidelined with the onset of the pandemic and stay-at-home orders. Most notably, our Events Committee chairperson, Molly McCowan, had sought to broaden the range of publishing-related conferences and other events the EFA attends—the primary goal of which is to attract clients who will use the Member Directory and post opportunities on the Job List. Unfortunately, most of those events were cancelled. Similarly, the EFA's local chapters, this year under the stewardship of Akiko Yamagata, provide a close and personal way to network and learn with our colleagues. Many chapters made the transition to online and virtual meetings, with varying levels of success. Even planning for our conference in 2021, another source of support for our members, was moved to the back burner this spring because of uncertainties surrounding when the world will be back to normal again.

Despite these setbacks, other committees achieved great successes. The Education program, this year led by Jennifer Lawler and picked up by Molly McCowan mid-year, continues to expand its offerings of skill-based and business-focused classes and webinars. The Discussion List, overseen by Sheila Buff, found a home on Groups.io (goodbye, Yahoo!), where members connect and share ideas, much like the early members did fifty years ago (but without the rotary dial phone). Sheila also led the EFA's advertising effort, generating print and digital advertising to expand our visibility into a broader span of markets in which our members specialize.

Diversity Initiative co-chairperson Sangeeta Mehta continued the important work of connecting and supporting EFA members with educational and professional resources for diversity, equity, and inclusion. She also heads the PR effort. Michael Coffino worked to expand membership benefits for our members, and Robin Martin, as Publications Committee chairperson, coordinated a 2020 booklet campaign with IngramSpark as our new distributor.

Keeping track of all EFA events and programs, and getting the news and other important information out to our members, were Denise Larrabee, who edits the *What's New at the EFA* ebulletin; Ruth Mullen and Tara Kovach, who anchor our expanding social media presence (with Ruth chairing our new Social Media Committee); and newsletter editor

Ruth E. Thaler-Carter, who continues to produce the *Freelancer*—one of the few ways we still communicate with members (only those who request it) via "snail mail."

We must add to this list of activities and accomplishments the completion of our new, comprehensive, survey-based rates chart—the culmination of years of work by Sangeeta Mehta and a small subcommittee of volunteers—and the updating of our organization's by-laws, led by co-executives Bill Keenan and Christina M. Frey. Despite the letdowns and setbacks, we have a lot to be proud of this year.

So, this is not only a milestone year for the organization; the EFA has plenty to celebrate within our current programs, thanks to our dedicated volunteers—who are too numerous to name, but still represent a very small percentage of our membership. As was true fifty years ago, twenty-five years ago, ten years ago, our organization is only as strong as the people who maintain and build it.

As we look back at the EFA's history in this commemorative booklet and glean some wisdom from the past, please take note of the names you will see, many of them over and over, and thank these people for building and maintaining the stable foundation on which we move into the future. The EFA has proven again and again that our members can depend on each other for support and community in the most difficult of times.

Christina M. Frey

William Keenan Jr.

Editorial Freelancers

1970 Employees from Grove Press strike.

1974 A group of freelancers begin meeting in each other's homes. Member Directory offered to members of the group.

1976 Meetings move to St. Mark's Church-in-the-Bowery. The group has 100 members and Publications, Benefits, and Structure committees.

1977 Formally named Editorial Freelancers Association. Begins issuing newsletter.

1979 EFA opens its first office on East 20th Street in Manhattan. Structure committee writes bylaws and creates the Board of Governors. First educational classes offered.

1981 Job Phone developed. EFA is incorporated.

1983 EFA buys its first computer.

1985 First office manager hired.

1989 Move to E. 23rd St. off Park Ave. First Affinity Group (for nonfiction magazine writers) launched. First chapters outside of New York formed in PA and NJ.

1991 First Rates Survey conducted (then known as Business Practices Survey).

1993 First EFA conference hosted at the Williams Club in NYC.

1995 Newsletter renamed the *Freelancer*. First professional discount offered to EFA members. Membership reaches 1,000.

1997 EFA initiates regional chapter development. First EFA website launched.

Association 1970-2020

2000 Discussion List launched.

2003 Member Directory now offered online.

2007 EFA begins offering booklets printed-on-demand, and also electronic versions.

2014 Monthly eBulletin titled What's New at the EFA launched. Job List postings surpass 5,000.

2017 Diversity Initiative is launched. New website and branding brought online.

2020 In April, EFA offers free webinars to members in response to the COVID-19 pandemic. Job List surpasses 8,700 job listings. The organization reaches 2,768 members.

1999 EFA switches the Job Phone to a Job List.

2002 First year offering videotaped Educational offerings

2005 Second EFA conference held, in New York.

2010 EFA begins using social media (Facebook, LinkedIn, and Twitter). Attends Book Expo America for the first time. A group to handle EFA event participation is established.

2016 Third EFA conference held in New York. Current Advertising committee formed. A PR group is established. FFA Twitter reaches 5,000 followers.

2019 Fourth EFA conference held, in Chicago. EFA joins Instagram. EFA Facebook reaches 10,000 followers.

1.
What Is the EFA?

As many of our members will tell you, the EFA is much more than "The Right Editor. Right Away." This is the advertising tagline we adopted, along with our new branding and website over the last decade. Editorial Freelancers Association members are editors, writers, indexers, proofreaders, researchers, desktop publishers, translators, and others who offer a broad range of skills and specialties. Members of the EFA are part of the largest and oldest national professional organization of editorial freelancers. We agree with our marketing copy that there's no better place to find the right editor (or publishing professional), right away!

The EFA is a national not-for-profit—501(c)6—organization, headquartered in New York City, run almost entirely by member volunteers, all of whom are also freelancers experienced in a wide range of professional skills, subject areas, and media. Begun in 1970 and incorporated in 1981, it is an international organization, whose members live and work all over the United States and in more than a dozen nations abroad.

The Board of Governors oversees the EFA's operations and keeps the membership informed of developments within the association. Annual elections of officers and members at large are held May through June, and the candidates' statements for upcoming elections are published on the-efa.org website. The board consists of four officers (two co-executives, a secretary, and a treasurer), members at large, and committee chairpersons. Members at large are elected to represent the interests of a broad base of members, to assist other governors and committees with EFA business, and to promote the EFA to members, potential members, and the publishing industry.

Behind the Scenes, but Making a Big Impact

The EFA is able to offer so many worthwhile benefits to its members through the hard work of volunteers, some of whom serve on the board. These volunteers are organized into committees, a system that goes back to the early years of the EFA with the formation of the Planning Committee.[1] This committee was concerned primarily with increasing membership, providing benefits, and meeting EFA's financial needs.

There are ten active committees today. These committees work as a team under the direction of two co-executives. The first to serve in this role were Elaine Chubb (1979–80) and Charles Carmony (1979–82). Today, the EFA runs smoothly under the leadership of Christina M. Frey (2016–current) and William Keenan Jr. (2013–current).

The history of the organization is a colorful one, and the story is eloquently told by those who were there in the four articles that follow chapter two. Fifty years ago, the group that originally came together were newly unemployed editors in NYC, struggling to make sense of changes in the publishing industry.

As the group grew, dues were initiated. In 1982, annual dues were $40. The executive committee of the board met during the summer of 2005 and recommended to the full board a budget that required increases in dues because of projected deficits. The EFA raised dues and fees as follows: Those who lived in the city of New York saw their dues increase from $115 to $125 for one year and from $215 to $225 for two years. For those who lived outside the city's boundaries, dues increased from $95 to $105 for one year and from $175 to $190 for two years.

---

1 EFA: 25 Years of Service to the Editorial Profession, pp. 7–8

Annual dues were raised just once since, and eliminated the distinction between NYC residents and others. In 2020, dues are $145 for one year or $260 for two years, and the dues now include the Job List.

The EFA community has continued to grow and thrive over the past twenty-five years.

Year	Number of Members
1995	1,000
2005	1,391
2015	2,299
2020	2,768

Many committees have been formed over the fifty-year history of the EFA, and through the hard work of the chairpersons and members of these committees, the membership of the EFA has become a community with numerous benefits. Members receive discounts on EFA courses designed to build and enhance editorial skills. They have exclusive access to the EFA newsletter and the Discussion List. Members also receive early notice of new publications written by and for editorial freelancers; invitations to networking meetings and speaker presentations; access to our Job List service; and special prices on Shake Law, PerfectIt, IngramSpark, and other indispensable resources. Most importantly, members get the opportunity to connect with other editorial freelancers. We learn from each other, support each other, and cheer each other on.

The EFA does not directly offer health insurance, although once upon a time it did; however, members can access healthcare discount plans through our third-party providers in some areas of the United States.

Neither does the EFA offer legal support to members, nor does it support any political causes; but it does support many of the organizations that have the resources to serve as advocates for their members, including the Authors Guild, ASJA, and National Writers Union. The EFA also offers a Code of Fair Practice, published originally by the Freelance Editorial Association, which merged with the EFA in 2000.

A pioneer in organizing freelancers into a network for mutual support and advancement, the EFA is now recognized throughout the publishing industry as *the* source for professional editorial assistance. And as editorial freelancing—indeed, freelancing in many fields of endeavor—becomes more prevalent, the association is looking at an even brighter future.

2.
EFA Employees

In 1979, the EFA opened its first office: a small space in a funky building on East 20th Street in Manhattan. According to Sheila Buff, the office was furnished with donations and cast-offs, including an antique partners' desk found on the street. In 1985, the EFA hired a series of temporary office managers, until the first long-term officer manager, David Bell, came on board.

In 2020, the EFA is fortunate to have the resources to employ one full-time staff member and two part-time staffers, without whom the board members and committee chairpersons would have a nearly impossible job.

The staff tasks are divided three ways: Events and Communications; Membership and Programs; and General Management.

In mid-March 2020, these employees, who generally work in the EFA office in the Media Law Research Center's space in midtown Manhattan, had to figure out how to do their jobs from home. Like the majority of the people they work for, our staff became remote workers. Their flexibility and resilience is remarkable, and from the point of view of those volunteers and members who rely on them every day for a variety of tasks, it was as if nothing had changed at all. Though surely it must have been a trying time for them, they apparently managed their work, their families, and the inconveniences of the pandemic without a hitch. They tell us their stories in their own voices below, which will no doubt serve as a valuable resource for historians of the 2020 pandemic.

ROBIN MARTIN AND DENISE LARRABEE

Vina Orden, Events and Communications Coordinator:

I work part-time as the EFA's Events and Communications Coordinator (from 9 a.m. to 6 p.m. on Mondays and Fridays and 1 p.m. to 6 p.m. on Tuesdays through Thursdays). Prior to the pandemic, I assisted Events Chair Molly McCowan in researching and registering for sponsorships of industry conferences and events nationwide. I coordinated with local chapters to recruit volunteers and provide them with display and marketing materials for the EFA booth at those events. Since the pandemic, many events the EFA traditionally sponsored have moved online entirely, so I (along with event professionals around the world) have had to adapt to an evolving virtual environment, increasingly working with graphic designers on digital marketing collateral and with different virtual conference platforms. This knowledge from other events can only be helpful as planning for the EFA's 2021 conference is underway.

These days, the communications aspect of my job has ramped up—I've found that many potential clients and members who call in are not looking just to have their queries answered, but also for reassurance from a human connection in these challenging times. I've also provided support to the board and other volunteers as they've created additional resources to help members—from updating the EFA website and sending email tips for working from home or the monthly Create-a-Word contest; to regularly publicizing on the EFA's LinkedIn company page our chapter and EFA-wide virtual events, webinars and courses, and the latest resources, such as the new and re-released booklets and the Resources for New Freelance Editors page on the website; to helping moderate some of the free monthly webinars for members.

Especially in a cramped New York City apartment, it can be challenging to navigate Zoom meetings and calls with my partner, who is an educator and has been teaching remote classes live. Currently, without an ergonomic workspace and access to a gym, I have to remind myself to tear myself away from computer, phone, and ebook screens and at least take one walk every day! Keeping work and living "spaces" (albeit mental rather than physical) separate also has been difficult, so both my partner and I have to be more conscious about disconnecting on evenings and weekends. That said, I'm grateful for the hour recouped from my daily commute to do some writing (or catch up on sleep)!

Christina Shideler, Membership and Programs Coordinator:

I also work part-time, 9 a.m. to 2 p.m. Monday through Friday, as the EFA's Membership and Programs Coordinator. Before the pandemic, I came into the office each day after a 40-minute commute that mixed a 15-minute walk across the bridge connecting Brooklyn to Queens with a short subway ride into Manhattan. Since my work primarily revolves around our all-virtual Education Program and addressing the concerns and questions of members, potential members, and potential clients, the nature of my work has not changed dramatically, but the volume has!

My work has been uncharacteristically busy in these six months under the pandemic. I think it is a mixture of increased interest from potential members who may be attracted to freelancing after losing in-house jobs due to the economic downturn, plus members with more time to finally ask questions that the pre-pandemic pace had pushed to the bottom of too-long lists.

I work primarily on my couch, as our rather small one-bedroom Brooklyn apartment doesn't give much room for an office, but will soon be relocating to Eastern Pennsylvania temporarily where my dog, husband, and I will have more room to spread out and experience the joys of nature that quarantined urban life doesn't grant us. Since I struggle with chronic illness, the lack of a commute has been a blessing, allowing me to conserve the energy that was formerly used for getting to the office.

Susannah Driver-Barstow, General Manager

I'm the EFA's sole full-time staffer. For my first several years on the job I was also the sole staffer, and I've welcomed adding wonderful colleagues Christina and Vina as the EFA membership and programming have grown. Before this position I was a freelancer and before that a staff editor at publishing houses. I discovered the EFA when looking to hire freelance copyeditors for the Feminist Press, back when the Job List was the Job Phone.

At the start of the Covid-19 pandemic, after organizing the staff's transition to working remotely, I worked at home in the Bronx from the bedroom my daughter had vacated while at college. In midsummer my husband, daughter, the family cat, and I were able to relocate to upstate New York, and we're all grateful for having a bit more room for the duration. My office is now an as-yet-undecorated study. I miss the very large wall map of the United States I've had on my EFA office walls for eight or nine years, dotted with pushpins for all the active chapters, even though I can, and do, go to the website and see a very lovely digital version of this.

Although we can't recreate our physical offices at home, staff stays in touch. Our weekly in-person staff meeting became a shorter but daily meeting on Zoom. We continue to use our excellent project management/collaboration program, Asana. And, of course, we have frequent use of email and we also text and even call each other on occasion. We use Groups.io to communicate with Board and member groups within the EFA, as well as email and the phone.

One of us goes in to the office about every two weeks to check on it, to collect mail, to mail tote inserts or other event materials (now much less frequently than pre-pandemic, but we're glad that some events, albeit in altered formats, are able to continue), and to retrieve information from the files and archives there that is needed for current work or for fiftieth anniversary projects.

The increase in the organization's need for staff support since the pandemic began (such as for the clearly needed new free monthly webinar series for members, which has seen record registration numbers) continues a recent expansion of staffing needs at the EFA. We now support twenty Board members, about fifteen major programs, thirty chapters, and more than 2,800 members and I have just hired another part-time staffer to help our phenomenal volunteers keep all of this humming. In this time of deep change and uncertainty from the pandemic, climate crises, economic upheaval, and the protests for racial justice, it's perhaps especially meaningful to be looking back at the past 50 years and recognizing the growth of the EFA into an enduring institution for freelancers within the communications and publishing industries.

The EFA Board of Governors is so grateful for the hard work and dedication of the EFA staff. They are very taxed right now, and Susannah has just hired a part-time office staff member to join the team. It's exciting to see the organization growing, and these paid staffers are crucial to the process.

3.

The Very Early Years,

by Elliot Linzer

Elliott Linzer is one of the EFA's longest-standing and more colorful members. He earns his living as a freelance indexer and has been a member of the EFA since 1976. He served on the national staff of the March on Washington for Jobs and Freedom in 1963; was a draft resister during the Vietnam War; and is currently active in Science for the People. This essay was first published as "The 'Prenatal' History of the EFA" by Elliot Linzer in the January–February 2020 issue of the Freelancer (Vol. 45, No. 1).

Looking at the current EFA, it is hard to imagine that the organization started out as a small group of political radicals meeting to support organizing a labor union of publishing workers. The mythology of the EFA's origin is that we started as a group supporting the striking employees of Grove Press in 1970. Well, yes and no. Yes, the founders of the EFA were all involved in those strike support actions in 1970. The problem is that about a half-dozen different organizations can trace their roots to those meetings. All of the other organizations were political, and most were ad hoc and had brief lifetimes.

I may not remember the exact names of these organizations, but they included Publishing Workers against the War in Vietnam, the Publishers

Committee for the Impeachment of Richard Nixon, and several other groups long forgotten.

The meetings that specifically led to the formation of an organization of freelancers started a bit later, around 1974, but did involve many of the same people.

The meetings supporting the Grove Press strike of 1970 included in-house workers, authors, freelancers, and others (outside the publishing industry) who felt a strong political commitment to organizing everybody in the publishing industry.

To digress a bit, the Grove Press strike was not simply a matter of conflicts between workers and their bosses, but involved at least three factions among the workers, with different analyses and demands, which sometimes coalesced and other times conflicted with each other. There were Grove Press workers who just wanted a better deal from their big leftist publisher and made traditional economic demands. There were also feminists, including Robin Morgan, a former Grove Press employee as well as a best-selling author, who wanted to see Grove Press publications present a more-feminist analysis and less pornography. Then there were the cultural revolutionaries, with an analysis that was completely different from those of the other two factions.

The lines between these three groups were not always clear, and some individuals straddled the ideological lines between them. These different factions of Grove Press workers were reflected in the group supporting the strike.

By 1974, the ad hoc committees opposing the Vietnam War and supporting the impeachment of Nixon had come and gone, but the group of publishing workers continued to meet and centered around freelancers, not staff employees. The four women credited with being the EFA's founding mothers were Faith Sale, Louise Stallard, Mary Heathcote, and Margaret Wolf. Cicely Nichols joined soon after. All five were self-consciously political, with strong leftist backgrounds and experience in the civil rights, anti-war, and labor movements. Others soon joined the group; most, but not all, from the same left backgrounds. Later additions included Mary Barnett and Jeannine Ciliotta, neither of whom were political. While these women, and others in the early group, all shared common values, they had major disagreements over strategy.

In the early years (1974 to February 1977), the group of freelancers did not have a name and met secretly. New members were recruited only by invitation. One of the major disagreements was over whether the group should announce its existence publicly. There was good reason for the secrecy: Blacklists still existed in the industry—this writer was blacklisted after the failed strike at Macmillan in 1974—and going public meant a risk of exposing all the members to potential blacklisting and other sanctions. The group prepared a mimeographed list of members and circulated it at each meeting, but marked it "confidential."

The meetings eventually became too large for the living rooms of the group's founders. I believe it was around 1976 that meetings moved to local churches, starting with St. Mark's Church-in-the-Bowery (on Second Avenue and East 10th Street in Manhattan).

The first meeting I attended, in October 1976, was held there, and Nichols was one of two main speakers. The other was her Legal Services attorney, who represented her in her claim for unemployment insurance after McGraw-Hill had stopped sending her freelance editing assignments. Nichols was denied the compensation when she applied for unemployment insurance; then, she appealed the decision to a New York State Department of Labor appeals board, which ruled in her favor. While the appeals board decision benefited her, it did not set a precedent and didn't directly help anyone else. Very simply, decisions of the New York State Department of Labor appeals board do not set or follow precedents.

Even without a name or any bylaws, the secret organization of freelancers had something of a structure and regular meetings—lots of meetings—too many meetings. First, there were the monthly membership meetings, with a speaker or panel of speakers; then, the members would break down into small groups for more personal discussions. The group each person attended was determined semi-randomly by a card they received from a deck of playing cards distributed at the beginning of the meeting. By prearrangement, at least one experienced member was in each small group. There was always somebody to initiate new members into the group.

Programs for the monthly membership meetings were determined by a Planning Committee, which also met once a month.

Membership in the Planning Committee was open to everybody. There also were committees for Benefits, Publications, and Structure (which I chaired), each with its own schedule of regular meetings. An active member of the group could attend three or four different meetings each month.

By February 1977, it was decided that the whole organization should decide what the group's name should be and whether it should go public. We voted on these issues at a general monthly meeting. The Editorial Freelancers Association became the name, and we decided to announce our existence to the outside world. The group started to grow very quickly. Some of the tactical differences that had been in the group all along caused some friction at Planning Committee and Structure Committee meetings. While everybody in the group seemed to agree that we needed to have some "clout" in the industry, exactly what that meant and how it could be achieved was in dispute.

Some members wanted the EFA to eventually become a union of freelancers, while others saw it as a professional association. I don't think anyone opposed the idea of a union, but many, including me, feared that we did not have enough support to move quickly in that direction.

Later in 1977, the EFA split into two organizations, with Faith Sale and Margaret Wolf (both former Grove Press employees), along with David Sachs (who had been a teacher, then an editor at Macmillan who was fired during the 1974 strike there), splitting off from the EFA to form a new group with a similar name, Freelance Editorial Workers Association, Inc. (FEWA). They made some grandiose promises (including a health plan to cover freelancers all over the United States), but that splinter group did not last long, vanishing after holding only two or three meetings.

The EFA was then on the road to becoming a professional association, not a union.

In retrospect, the fears of the EFA's founders—that there was a risk of possible retaliatory actions against the membership once we went public—were misplaced. The EFA started to grow and has continued to thrive over its forty-five-year (or forty-nine-year) history.

Sources

Kohl, Martin. "EFA's History: Volunteers Made It Happen." In *EFA: Twenty-Five Years of Service to the Editorial Profession*, 7–10. New York: Editorial Freelancers Association, 1995.

Linzer, Elliot. "A Tribute to Cicely Nichols." The *Freelancer* 31, no. 1 (September–October 2006): 7.

Rogers, Trumbull. "How We Began." The *Freelancer* 31, no. 1 (September–October 2006): 3, 7.

4.

Volunteers Made It Happen: 1976–1995,

by Martin Kohl

Martin Kohl (1944–2003) was an active EFA member and served as a member at large on the board in 1994–1995, wrote the EFA publication "The Freelancer's Bookshelf" in 1994, and reported often for the Freelancer. This essay first published as "EFA's History: Volunteers Made It Happen," in EFA: Twenty-Five Years of Service to the Editorial Profession, New York: Editorial Freelancers Association, 1995.

By 1976, the EFA had 100 members and was holding its general meetings in a school cafeteria in New York City's Greenwich Village. The leadership group, called the Planning Committee, was concerned primarily with increasing membership, providing benefits, and meeting the EFA's financial needs. The organization also produced a rudimentary Member Directory and a monthly newsletter.

During the late 1970s, the EFA continued to grow steadily. It became clear that a more formal structure was needed. Organizing that structure took two years. A Structure Committee wrote bylaws and created the

Board of Governors, which was to be headed by two co-executives, one female and the other male. It also created the positions of secretary and treasurer.

Charles Carmony, an indexer, and Elaine Chubb, a copyeditor, were the first two co-executives.

By holding general meetings in a variety of places, such as the Carnegie Center, Women's City Club, and Stephen Wise Free Synagogue, and using a mail drop and answering service in the Flatiron Building at 175 Fifth Avenue, the EFA was able to increase its membership to the point where enough revenue was available to rent an office. Finding an office had become a top priority: The EFA needed a place to keep membership records and receive mail.

In 1979, the EFA opened its first office, a small, dark space in a funky building on East 20th Street in Manhattan. It was furnished with a combination of luck and charity. "We found some furniture in the office we moved into, and some came from a vacant office across the hall. The landlord told us to help ourselves. We also found some of it in the street," says Rogers. The EFA now had somewhere to offer courses, hold board and committee meetings, and keep its records.

Within a few years, the organization outgrew the 20th Street office and moved to bigger and brighter quarters—with more reliable heat and adequate wiring for air conditioning—on East 23rd Street. With the move came a new computer system and a more professional approach to office management. The new space was large enough to hold twenty to thirty people comfortably, allowing the EFA to hold courses and affinity group meetings without having to arrange for outside space. However, general meetings continued to be held in more ample spaces like the nearby Women's City Club.

Even though the EFA is still using some of the same furniture that was scrounged for its first office—in particular, a massive mahogany partners' desk that is very hard to move—the association's headquarters on West 23rd Street is indicative of how far it has come. The offices consist of a spacious central area for general meetings and three smaller rooms housing the business office, a library, and committee files and mail bins.

In 1985 came the novel (for the EFA) idea of hiring an office manager to answer the phone, deal with the mail, and handle the variety of chores required by a professional organization. But even more important were two innovations that came from volunteers. The first, the Job Phone, was modeled after a similar service run by Washington Independent Writers

(WIW). Instead of charging a percentage from each job a freelancer got from the service, as WIW and other groups did, the EFA decided to charge subscribers a flat, one-time fee of $10, now $20 [and in 2020 included in membership dues –ed.] which can usually be earned back in the first hour of an assignment. The Job Phone's founder, Trumbull Rogers, suggested the idea to the Board of Governors, then set up the service and ran it from October 1981 until June 1988, by which time there were nearly 400 subscribers.

Although the availability of work is obviously vital for freelancers, knowing what the market wants is equally important. Affinity groups for members working in such fields as medical editing, computers, textbooks, desktop publishing, and public relations were begun in 1989, when medical writer and former Program Committee chair Walter Alexander began the first such group, for nonfiction magazine writers. Meeting about once a month, each affinity group features speakers discussing topics ranging from what kind of ideas a magazine might be looking for to the latest computer software for indexers. The value of having an editor or a director of communications discuss a company's editorial needs is inestimable, as is the ability to question that person more closely after the presentation.

Affinity groups for new freelancers (who may, in fact, already have many years of editorial experience) provide the neophyte independent contractor with the basic skills and knowledge that can make the difference between success and failure. "I think it's a really important part of the experience for a lot of people and it's unleashed a lot of creativity. In the past few years, Affinity Groups have been a major factor in our growth and provided an impetus for moving to our new offices," comments Program Committee chair Sheila Buff.

All of the innovations, leadership, and plain hard work that have kept the EFA growing for the last twenty-five years came from volunteers. Some freelanced for a while and went back to full-time positions; others continued freelancing on a permanent basis. As Rogers points out, the freelance life doesn't suit everyone; some people prefer the structured environment of an office, or can't deal with the uncertainties of freelancing. But whatever their preference, the freelancers in the EFA have always managed to find time for their organization. "A core group of about fifty or sixty volunteers year after year were the ones you could count on to really pull the weight and do the work and keep the organization running and growing."

The EFA was a pioneer in organizing freelancers into a network for mutual support and advancement. Today it is recognized throughout the publishing industry as the source for professional editorial assistance. And as editorial freelancing—indeed, freelancing in many fields of endeavor—becomes more prevalent, the EFA can look forward to an even brighter future.

5.

How We Began,

by J. Trumbull Rogers

J. Trumbull Rogers (1939-2013) served as EFA co-executive director and treasurer, and initiated the Job Phone service, precursor to today's Job List. This essay was first published in the September-October 2006 issue of the Freelancer (Vol. 31, No. 1).

Thirty-six years ago, in the winter of 1970, "editors at Grove Press went on strike in an effort to make the publishing industry more responsive to their needs. Two Grove editors who found themselves freelancing again—Mary Heathcote and Cicely Nichols—met with freelancers Faith Sale, Louise Stallard, and Margaret Wolf to discuss the situation, and predicaments, of freelancers" (from a letter from Cicely Nichols to Trumbull Rogers and Martin Kohl, Sept. 1999). As any long-time EFA member knows, this is the short version of how the present organization was born. Of this group of Founding Mothers, four (Mary Heathcote, Louise Stallard, Margaret Wolf, and Faith Sale) have died, and one—Cicely Nichols—is alive, though it has recently come to the attention of the EFA's Board of Governors that she is seriously ill. [Cicely Nichols died in 2008 -ed.]

It is probably a good idea to recount the story of the EFA's founding every few years, so newer members can become aware of our origin, and to remind the rest of us of how we began. Like many organizations, our beginning was small and uncertain. However, that first meeting must have struck a chord, because, as Carol L. O'Neill and Avima Ruder wrote in *The Complete Guide to Editorial Freelancing* (Barnes & Noble Books, 1974, now out of print), "Freelancers on occasion complain of loneliness, of being cut off from the mainstream of publishing—and from human contact. There is no organization where freelancers can meet to talk shop and exchange experiences, to share triumphs and gripes." In fact, at the time, this book was the only centralized source of information about the editorial freelancing profession, a role that the EFA was already assuming and expanding. Of course, when we became aware of this phrase, we wrote the publisher, and the next printing duly contained a mention of our existence. In fact, when I joined the EFA in 1977, freelancers still fiercely guarded such information as the names of their clients and the rates they charged—even where to find editorial flags, which editors used for queries and comments before the 3-M Company invented Post-Its. It was this barrier of paranoia that the EFA eventually broke down. However, this is only part of the debt editorial freelancers owe to Cicely and her colleagues, who set the tone when they came together to discuss their situation and share information.

Yet the EFA's continued existence was by no means assured by the fact of those early meetings.

As word of what they were up to began to spread from friend to friend, more and more freelancers showed up until the nascent group outgrew people's apartments. Then, in 1977, attempts to unionize Macmillan led to another strike, which in turn led to a schism in the EFA's leadership, because a group led by Sale, Wolf, and a former Macmillan editor named David Sachs, thought the EFA should become a union. As a result, they eventually founded a short-lived splinter organization—they held perhaps three meetings—which they called Freelance Editorial Workers Inc. Others in the EFA, including Nichols, Heathcote, Mary Barnett, and Jeannine Ciliotta, opposed this unionizing effort, feeling "the clout for a successful union was not present" (from Nichols's letter, 1999) and so establishing a stable organization first should be the goal.

When I joined the EFA, there were still those in the organization who were for turning the group into a union, but the prevailing opinion was that if we wanted to have any influence at all on publishers, we needed to become a responsible professional society, and to attract members, we had to offer services to the members, including a better place to network and socialize than the school cafeteria where the EFA was, at the time, holding its general meetings.

I can recall coming in contact with Cicely only twice after I joined. The first time was when I told Mary Barnett, a friend of Mary Heathcote's, that I wanted to do something in the organization. She suggested I talk to Cicely, who was at the time editing the newsletter. Cicely asked me to write an article on Mark Green's (then New York City's ombudsman) push to pass a law that all legal documents had to be written in plain English. The EFA's leadership thought such a law could result in work for freelance editors and proofreaders, but the article never materialized. Also about that time, after seven years of service to the EFA, Cicely decided to focus her energies on other aspects of her life. Then, a year or so after I became program co-chair with Dorothy Macdonald (an indexer), Cicely contacted me with an idea she had. This was the time of the Tall Ships, one of which was to be a replica of a small Revolutionary War ship, *Providence*, which had been part of Maryland's naval contribution to the cause. The *Providence* would be taking people on sails up the Hudson River, and Cicely offered to organize rides for EFA members, their friends, and families at a reduced rate. After that, although I'd hear about her from time to time, Cicely ceased all active participation in the EFA. This does not mean that she lost interest in the EFA and its progress, as attested by the 1999 letter, which she wrote after viewing the new EFA website.

By the time of her retirement, however, her ideas and other participation had helped the group move well on its way toward becoming a viable professional organization. There was still a way to go, but membership was expanding annually and the EFA was gaining the respect of publishers and their professional associations, including the American Association of University Presses (AAUP), with whom we put on a joint meeting. The first meeting I ran as program co-chair featured a talk by Herbert Mitgang, of the *New York Times*, who wrote about books and publishing, most notably articles opposing the increasing conglomeration in the industry. He mentioned the EFA in a subsequent column, which resulted in a surge in membership. But it was the EFA's focus on providing a place for members to socialize and exchange information—ideas that were the motivation for those five women to come together in 1970, and which Cicely and some others kept alive during the EFA's formative years—that have allowed the EFA to work and grow. This is why we need to remind ourselves of our origin and to continue to honor those who were there in the beginning.

6.

Parting Thoughts from a Long-Time Co-Exec, by J.P. Partland

J. P. Partland was an EFA co-executive from 2000 to 2016. This essay was first published in the July-August 2016 issue of the Freelancer (Vol. 40, No. 5).

I think I joined the EFA in 1997. At the time, I was looking to be part of a professional association.

While I had been availing myself of the ASJA's Contract volunteers, I didn't qualify to join their group as per their guidelines. And while I had been working full-time as a freelance writer for a few years, I was publishing much of my stuff on the web, which they didn't seem to regard as much.

I joined on the suggestion of a more-experienced friend who said he thought that having a prophylactic organization would be useful. He was writing porn at the time—a freelance music writer had to feed his family. I saw it as a way to learn how to be a better freelancer. To me, that meant being smarter about business: finding clients, dealing with clients, presenting myself better, protecting myself better, gaining a greater sense of the field and the issues relevant to freelancing. At the time, I was uninsured, and I was also hoping to find cheap health insurance. I never did acquire cheap health insurance, but I think I did gain everywhere else.

I went to meetings. There were at least a few meetings a month at the EFA offices back then. I "networked," which I guess is just a way of saying I was somewhat social. I used the Job Phone, which was a separate fee at the time, and you had to call in to listen to a long audio recording. I felt I was getting what I had wanted to get out of the EFA, although, as Sheila Buff, one of the co-execs at the time, said, "It's like a garbage can—you get out what you put in." She was also the person who convinced me to join the board.

I'm still getting what I want to get out of the EFA. I've scored one or two jobs from the Job List, but I hadn't joined for that. Even back then, when it was a separate fee, it was easy to see it as a benefit—a single job would pay for the service for many years, and it is always a possibility that the potential client might have another need at another time or recommend me to someone else.

For me, the EFA is about helping make freelancing easier for members, and maybe influencing the freelance editorial world for the better. By easier, I mean reducing the difficulty of the hustle. I'm not scouring websites for jobs: The EFA is making it easier for the jobs to find me. If I have questions about taxes or copyright or annoying clients, I have a place where I can post a query and the hive mind probably has an answer. While I haven't availed myself of Education offerings in a long time, I think of them in the same way: I have access if I want it.

Since I joined, many aspects of freelancing have changed dramatically. The EFA has changed dramatically as well. We have a much larger, geographically and skill-diverse membership. Our membership was in the low 900s when I joined, and I think close to 70 percent lived within the New York metropolitan area. Now, we're close to 2,500 members, and they live not only throughout the USA, but in several other countries and on a few other continents, too.

We have many fewer meetings at the office, but we're very busy online, whether it's the Discussion List or our classes. The Discussion List, in some ways, offers not only networking, big-picture job advice and granular help on things like nagging grammar queries, but a certain amount of socializing—the watercooler talk we don't get because we're shut off in our home offices.

I think the organization's growth makes it possible for the EFA to be more of a help, more influential, and more likely to make a positive difference in members' work lives. At first blush, it might seem that having more members means more people competing for the same jobs. I think that we're finding more jobs being listed, and more website and directory visitors, which means that it might actually get easier to have work find you. I also think that with more members, the organization's name is known to more people, which could lead more traffic to the EFA's site. There, with the rates chart, Code of Fair Practice, and sample contracts and invoices, we can influence the freelancing world as well as educate potential clients—another example of the organization making freelancing easier.

Another difference is that our size means we have the means, aka funding, to increase our visibility. And this is something we've been pursuing as of late. We've become a regular at Book Expo America, and are attending more and more conferences. We're spending more on advertising and marketing, both in standard and innovative ways. We're busy tweeting; we're active on Facebook. And we're in the midst of a website redesign and more. With the size and geographic diversity, though, comes a problem: disconnect. In terms of size, it's easier for members not to speak up about a problem or volunteer to do something, because there's an assumption that someone else already has it covered. When we're all online, it seems easier not to feel an obligation to help out. It's akin to the "slacktivism" criticism leveled at social media. You need to think about details, the big picture, the immediate and the long term to succeed at freelancing. I hope you're doing that not only for yourself, but for others as well.

The EFA is one place where your actions will benefit more than just yourself. Collective action is far more powerful than a single voice in the wilderness. And that can be hard when you're working for yourself and your only connection to a group is virtual.

This, in many ways, is a terrible time to step down from the co-exec's perch. Back when I first joined the board, the organization was in debt, we had little money to spend on initiatives, and we had fewer volunteers willing and able to lend a hand. Now, we're comfortably in the black, are pretty well plugged-in online and able to promote the organization in ways that were impossible only a short time ago. The board has risen to the challenge: I expect that the organization's visibility will grow, which is good for everyone.

Thanks for letting me pretend to be in charge these past 16 years. Excellent board members also did a great job on that front. You've done right by me. I hope I've done right by you. I hope that we can collectively continue to improve our individual lots.

7.
Creating a Community

One might say the history of the EFA is a history of its benefits. They certainly are the core reason the EFA exists, particularly the benefit of community. As Trumbull Rogers reminded us in 2006:

> It was the EFA's focus on providing a place for members to socialize and exchange information—ideas that were the motivation for those five women to come together in 1970, and which Cicely and some others kept alive during the EFA's formative years—that have allowed the EFA to work and grow.[2]

The EFA has certainly grown. Since its twenty-fifth anniversary in 1995, the EFA has seen substantial growth in three areas: the size of its membership, which went from 1,000+ to 2,800+; the amount of its expenses, which increased from $127,099 to $375,489; and the number and breadth of benefits it offers its members.

These benefits are more than something received for dues paid. Every EFA benefit requires volunteers to join together, work with each other, and learn from each other. When members take advantage of a benefit, they connect with and learn from their colleagues. Along the way, they create a community. For these reasons, it seems fitting that we use the EFA's benefits as the organizing principle in this telling of the EFA's

---

2 Rogers, How We Began

history, which will focus on the past twenty-five years and, at times, reach back even further.

The **Member Directory** (now online at the-efa.org) has been a resource for EFA members since the organization's inception in the 1970s. It began as a few typed pages and grew into a small bound book. The annual Member Directory originally listed members alphabetically and by skills, specialties, and geographic location. It was distributed free to all members and also circulated widely within the publishing industry.

The Member Directory became available online in 2003. In 2008, a new member database, integrated with the EFA website, was launched. With this database, members could maintain their own records and directory listing, and clients could search the database free of charge.

Today, this searchable database lists more than 240 search terms that clients can use to identify freelancers with the right combination of experience, knowledge, and skills for their project and learn how to contact them directly. Visitors can search the EFA Member Directory by editorial skill, style guide, subject specialty, genre, material, language, hardware and software capability, age or grade level of the project, location, name, keyword, or any combination of these. They can identify freelancers of interest and contact them directly through the information they provide. Members post their own descriptions of their services and expertise. Clients from every area of the publishing and communications industries, placement agencies, and unpublished and new authors can use the directory for free. Many members have reported getting good assignments from clients who hired them after searching the directory for freelancers with the skills and expertise they were seeking.

Where do you find your clients?

By referral (79%, 307 Votes)

Through your own marketing (43%, 165 Votes)

Through your directory listing with the EFA (40%, 154 Votes)

Through the EFA Job List (38%, 147 Votes)

Through social media (LinkedIn, Facebook, Twitter, other) (28%, 107 Votes)

Through your directory listing with another organization (22%, 86 Votes)

Through other job lists (12%, 47 Votes)

Through companies like Upwork (8%, 30 Votes)

Total Voters: **388**

Like the Member Directory, education in various forms has been a core benefit of joining the EFA from the beginning. In its early years, the EFA **Education Program** consisted of speakers or panels of speakers followed by discussion groups — all organized by members. By 1989, these discussion groups developed into Affinity Groups for members working in such fields as medical editing, computers, textbooks, desktop publishing, and public relations. The first (for nonfiction magazine writers) was started by Walter Alexander, then Program Committee chairperson. They met in person, in NYC and the surrounding areas, about once a month, and by 1995 were going strong. Affinity Groups recorded for that year were desktop publishing; grammar and usage; medical writing and editing; new freelancers; PR and advertising; young adult /children's books. Topics covered at their meetings included CD-ROMS and the future of publishing; opportunities in technical communications; and protecting your electronic rights. In 2000, a new Affinity Group, business practices, was added.

Seven years later, David R. Hall and Laurie Lewis, co-leaders of the Affinity Group called "freelancers approaching career transitions," reported that they were disbanding this group because of lack of interest, and noted the lack of interest in EFA Affinity Groups in general:

> Fifteen to 20 years ago, EFA's Affinity Groups could draw 30 to 40 attendees and often more, even without speakers, and general meetings often had more than 60 in attendance. Today, not just in EFA but in other groups in our experience, meeting attendance is down. We believe that "face time" is giving way to online exchanges as a means of networking in society as a whole, and not just among the young folks who came of age with computers.[3]

Affinity Groups seemed to have faded out completely by 2009. Fortunately, educational courses flourished. EFA classes started in 1979, when the EFA acquired office space at East 20th Street in Manhattan and thus had a place to hold classes. All classes were held in-person. In

---

3 Annual Report, 2007

1989, the organization moved to a building on East 23rd Street, which provided more space for larger class sizes and Affinity Group meetings.

Twenty-five years ago the EFA's Education Program was offering nine to twelve courses per year. These courses covered topics ranging from basic copyediting to writing proposals and grants, from organizing one's office to setting project rates. Participants had to join the in-person classes in NYC. Around 1988, Ruth E. Thaler-Carter started offering in-person EFA workshops about getting started in freelancing in Washington, D.C., as well as in NYC. In 2002, the EFA offered its first videotaped version of a course in the fall: Richard Adin's marketing seminar.

The advent of the internet and online learning platforms made it possible for the EFA to extend the important benefit of educational courses to more members nationwide. Under the leadership of Jen Maybin, the program grew exponentially. Today, the EFA hosts online, asynchronous courses (on the Sakai platform), real-time webinars (using GoToWebinar), and on-demand recorded webinars designed especially for freelance editors, writers, and other editorial specialists around the world. Topics still include those offered twenty-five years ago, but one can also register for courses on networking, setting your rates, children's literature, academic editing, and sensitivity reads. Courses are open to members and nonmembers and require advance registration.

Courses and webinars are offered throughout the year and revenue from educational offerings makes up 30 percent of EFA annual revenue. Latest data on registration for educational offerings records 1,324 registrants for 2018, a testament to how much the program has grown over the last twenty-five years.

Free Webinar Recordings

In response to the COVID-19 pandemic, in April 2020 the EFA offered three free webinars for members: Survival Tips for the Current Crisis, presented by Ruth E. Thaler-Carter; Preserving Mental Health in Times of Crisis, presented by Christina M. Frey; and Creative Ways to Find and Generate Income during Troubled Times, presented by Molly McCowan. Other free webinars offered to members throughout the year included Tech Tools for Writers and Editors, presented by Adrienne Montgomerie;

Sensitivity Reads: What You Need to Know to Offer This Service, presented by Lourdes Venard; and Building a Client Base to Weather Any Storm, presented by Molly McCowan.

Members expressed such a strong interest in the free webinars (many "sold out" at 250 participants) that the offerings will likely continue.

From its inception, the **Job List** has provided a system for potential clients to submit an ad and have freelancers who are interested contact them directly. The first effort to provide EFA members with employment opportunities, the Job Phone, was initiated in October 1981 by Trumbull Rogers. It was modeled after a similar service operated by Washington Independent Writers, but differed in one key aspect: Instead of charging a percentage from the earnings of each job a freelancer received from the service, subscribers paid a flat, one-time fee of $10, which was usually earned back by the freelancer with one hour of work on the assignment. Trumbull ran this phone-in service until June 1988, at which time there were nearly 400 subscribers.

By 1995, the fee for editors to participate in the Job List had increased to $20. The current service is included in the benefits EFA members receive with their annual dues, a system that began in 2011.[4]

To this very day, something that has remained the same is that each job post is hand-screened by a human. What has changed is that jobs are now posted on the website within twenty-four hours and emailed to members who request them.

The organization is proud to have many repeat clients—proof of how swiftly and effectively the EFA Job List targets our membership. We post jobs from every area of the publishing and communications industries, including staff jobs, jobs from placement agencies, and jobs from unpublished and new authors. We do not post low-paying or nonpaying jobs, jobs that pay by royalty or on spec, or internships of any sort.

In 1995, the Job List was posting two to five jobs per week, or eight to ten per month. In 1999, the EFA switched from a phone-in system to one in which members sign-up to receive emails of job listings. This led

---

4   EFA: *25 Years of Service to the Editorial Profession*, 9

to a significant increase, and by 2002, the total number of jobs posted for that year was 538. The Job List reached its highest number to date in 2006, with 700 job postings. Job Listings hit a milestone in 2012, when it reached a total of 5,000 jobs posted since its inception. In August 2020, the total jobs posted stands at 8,703.

EFA's Job List is a bellwether for the state of the job market for editorial freelancers, and the plethora of freelance job opportunities did not last due to the economic crisis of 2008. The number of job postings "fell off a cliff" beginning that July, according to Sheila Buff, EFA Job List Chair and Discussion List manager at the time. In 2009, the EFA posted only 252 jobs. A slow and steady rise began the following year, and in 2019, the EFA posted 630 jobs, with an average of 52 per month.

Typical postings in 1995 were from book, magazine, and textbook publishers, book packagers, nonprofit organizations, major corporations, and individuals.[5] Tracking conducted by Sheila Buff, beginning in September 2019, indicates a wide variety of job postings today. The following data categorize job postings from September 1 through December 31, 2019. Miscellaneous refers to the usual mixed bag of requests, e.g., compiling a bibliography or editing a personal statement.

Table 1 Job Postings September–December 2019

Academic/dissertation	36
Fiction	21
Miscellaneous**	21
STEM	12
Miscellaneous nonfiction books	16
Business/marketing	14
Educational materials	11
Memoir	10
Religious	8
YA/kid lit	6

---

5 (*25 Years*, 4)

Our **Discussion List** is where members share their vast experience and knowledge about the business of freelancing, tips on "fixing" knotty language problems, and suggestions for skill improvement. It is intended to be a list populated by professionals in the industry, or those working toward professional status. The number of moderators of the Discussion List has dwindled over the years, a problem that the board of governors continues to address in 2020. Discussion List moderator(s) must do a delicate dance to maintain freedom of expression and appropriate professional chat on this active platform.

EFA's online Discussion List was started in 1999 by Sheila Buff, a member of the EFA board of governors for more than twenty years who served as co-executive director from 1995 to 2001. By 2004, it consisted of 473 members with an average of 650 messages per month.[6] Buff reported an all-time record of 1,083 messages for the month of January 2008.[7] In 2017, the members subscribed to the Discussion List reached an all-time high of 1,961, but the number dropped sharply the following year. In early 2020, the EFA made the switch from Yahoo Groups to Groups.io, after an extended search for a new host platform. As of September 2020, there were 1,743 members of the Discussion List, which represents 59 percent of EFA's membership, and there have been more than 81,000 messages.

Number of members on the Discussion List
2008: 879
2010: 640
2012: 810
2014: 1,347
2016: 1,785
2018: 1,429
September 2020: 1,743

In 1997, the development of **regional chapters** was initiated to enrich the EFA experience for the increasing number of members outside the New York headquarters area. By 2002, the EFA had seven chapters

---

6 Annual Report, 2004
7 Annual Report 2009

(Atlanta, Boston, Indianapolis, Los Angeles, the mid-Hudson Valley, Philadelphia, and Seattle). This number more than doubled by 2010. "The caliber of speakers and topics has been impressive across the board," wrote Kristine Hunt, Chapter Development chairperson at that time. "Beyond professional development, several chapters have had wonderful social events, including regular Scrabble nights and holiday parties, and have been involved in writing and editing-related events, such as book festivals."[8]

In 2014, there were eighteen chapters, representing the EFA in almost every region of the United States.

With the introduction of the re-branded and re-designed website in 2017, news and activities from chapter coordinators became front and center, showcasing the opportunities for members across the US and internationally. Our first chapter on the continent of India launched that year.

Today, the EFA has regional chapters and networking groups all over the country, and new ones form as interest arises. Chapter events are open to all members, guests of members, and freelancers interested in joining the EFA.

The chairperson of the Chapter Development committee handles chapter development and management. Chapter meetings can be of an informal, networking-only nature or focused on a formal topic or speaker to provide continuing education and professional development of editorial freelancers. Each chapter, once established, has its own page on the EFA website, and each chapter coordinator (or coordinator team) is responsible for posting events there.

Members of chapters may also represent the organization at regional publishing or trade events, providing an opportunity to network with other EFA members and industry professionals. These events have included such gatherings as the Tucson Festival of Books, the Book Expo America, Digital Book World, the Self-Publishing Expo, and the Editors Association of Canada conference. In fact, the EFA Events committee

---

8 July/Aug *News* 2010 p. 5

began as a subcommittee of Chapter Development under the leadership of Robin Martin and Lindsay Alexander.

Today, EFA is proud to have 30 chapters.

Arizona/Southwest
Boston
Central Massachusetts
Chicago
Colorado
Connecticut
Florida
Georgia
Houston
Indiana
Los Angeles
Lower and Mid-Hudson Valley
Maryland
Michigan
New York City
North Carolina
Northern California
North Texas (DFW)
Ohio
Orange County, California
Philadelphia
Phoenix
Pittsburgh
Rochester
SE Wisconsin
SF/Bay Area
St. Louis
Upper Hudson, NY
Vermont
Virginia

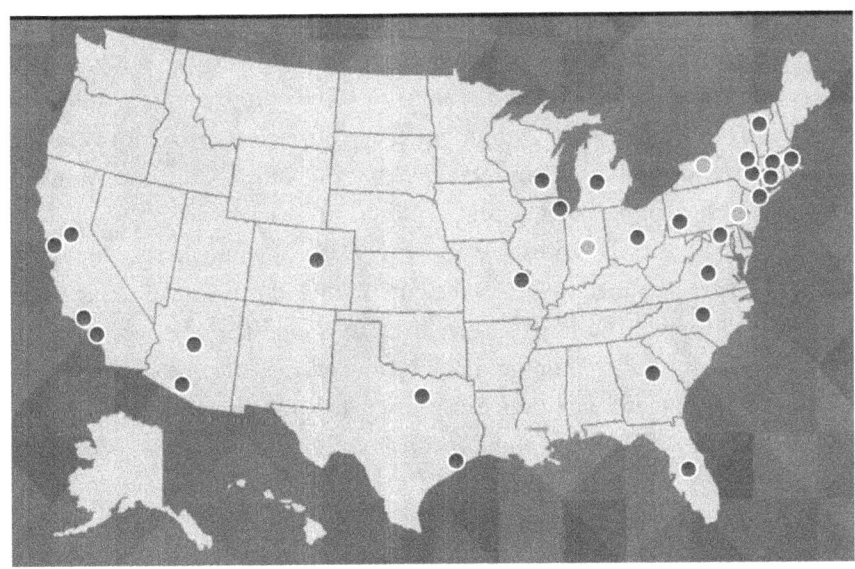

Besides chapter meetings and educational offerings, the EFA hosts **events** that give freelancers a variety of ways to network with other freelancers and industry professionals. **Meetings** may take place at NYC headquarters, at regional chapters across the country, or by webcast—something that was particularly useful during this year's unprecedented COVID-19 pandemic. Over the years, these **meetings and events** have included expert panels, special guest speakers, the annual business meeting, and joint meetings with related organizations. On the lighter side, the EFA holds networking lunches, Scrabble nights, coffee hours, picnics, and holiday parties at the New York headquarters and at many chapters.

Periodically, the EFA holds a national **professional conference** in different locations in the United States. The EFA's first conference, "Secrets of Successful Freelancing," was held at the Williams Club in NYC in 1993. Twelve years later, another was held, also in New York: "Be a Better Freelancer: Take Your Business to New Heights." This conference was chaired by Ruth E. Thaler-Carter. Seventy-five EFA members attended this one-day conference offering several speakers and classes.

In 2016, under the leadership of Laurie Lewis, the EFA held the conference once again in New York. It was after this conference that the EFA made a commitment to host future conferences in different parts of the country. And in 2019, the EFA conference was held in Chicago. EFA conferences have evolved to gather freelance editors, writers, indexers, translators, and other editorial professionals to network with colleagues and develop professionally. Session topics included skills development, the business of freelancing, and working with clients.

In 2010, the EFA embarked on a new marketing initiative by appearing at Book Expo America (BEA), the publishing industry's major trade show, held in May at the Javits Center in Manhattan. The goal, according to Sheila Buff, was "to promote the Job List and the [Member] Directory to the publishing industry as an efficient way to find freelance help." The EFA shared a booth with Josephine Bacon from London, who was there representing her translation company. "The event was reasonably successful for us," wrote Buff, "particularly given that it was our first time and that the booth was in Writers' Row, distinctly off the main path for show visitors."[9]

---

9 Annual Report 2010

Since then, formation of the EFA **Events Committee** has assured that the organization continues to attend, display, and be represented at industry events every year since to promote the Job List and attract new members. As of last year, that list of industry events has grown to nineteen. The events the EFA participates in include book festivals and trade conferences that are opportunities for promoting the organization to the publishing industry and the public. Recently, the organization has been making an extra effort to assure a presence where under-represented writers and editors can learn about us and might be encouraged to join our ranks. Volunteer EFA members work with the Events Committee chairperson and help staff the EFA booth at these events.

Until 2017, the Events Committee was a subcommittee of the Chapter Development Committee. The move to involve more EFA members as representatives of the organization was designed to spread the word about everything we have to offer. A side benefit was that regional chapter members were provided with an opportunity to network amongst themselves and with professionals in the industry for whom they might be able to provide a service.

Many 2020 events were cancelled due to the COVID-19 pandemic. In 2019, the EFA exhibited at these events:
- ACES, Providence
- American Medical Writers Association Annual Conference, San Diego
- American Society of Journalists and Authors, New York
- AWP, Portland, OR
- Baltimore Book Festival
- BookExpo and BookCon, New York
- Boston Book Festival
- Brooklyn Book Festival, New York
- Dallas-Fort Worth Writers Conference
- LA Times Festival of Books
- Mountain of Authors, Colorado Springs
- The Muse & the Marketplace, Boston
- The Native American Literature Symposium, Prior Lake, MN
- Portland Book Festival
- Romance Writers of America Conference, New York

- Romance Writers of America, New England Chapter Conference, Burlington
- ThrillerFest, New York
- WORDfest, Hurst, TX
- Writer's Digest, New York

The EFA issues several types of **publications** for its members, including the bimonthly newsletter the *Freelancer*, the monthly ebulletin *What's New at the EFA*, and various booklets on topics of interest to freelancers. While the ebulletin functions as a resource for members to keep current on EFA activities, the content of the *Freelancer* is almost entirely member-generated (and unlike the rest of the EFA's publications, which use the Chicago Manual of Style and our own customized style sheets, the *Freelancer* uses AP style). EFA members are also invited to submit proposals for the Booklets Program, which publishes booklets on specialized topics of professional interest to editorial freelancers.

The EFA has published a newsletter either monthly or bimonthly continuously since at least 1977. Known simply as *News!*, the newsletter was renamed **the *Freelancer*** in 1995 and completely redesigned by Mary Ratcliffe, newsletter production editor at the time, following previous newsletter editors Anita Mondello and Oona O'Sullivan. Mary's report that year gives insight into the topics covered throughout the '90s:

> We have tried to apportion coverage among all the professional interests of our members, keeping in mind that many of you wear several hats. Thus, we run stories about editing, writing, computers, research public relations, and anything else that germane to helping our members develop and expand their freelance careers. Business issues are covered regularly, notably in Charles Buckley's column about taxation and Patricia Godfrey's updates on computer options and resources. We try to keep our readers informed about prizes, conferences, and courses available to them, as well as about governmental initiatives that may affect them for good or ill.[10]

---

10 Sept/Oct 1995 *News*, pp. 4–5

The *Freelancer* was redesigned again in 2007, when board member Ruth E. Thaler-Carter became the editor, a position she holds to this day. In her words, she "made some minor adjustments in the look of the newsletter while retaining the original overall format, with the goal of making it more visually interesting, lively and readable, and of giving members more visibility for their contributions."[11] She also began publishing book reviews by Marie Shear (1940–2017), which appeared regularly and have been indexed and are available to members on the EFA website.

EFA members receive the *Freelancer* newsletter as a benefit of membership. It focuses on information of professional value to freelancers and is published six times a year. The *Freelancer* provides articles about freelance and communications/publishing trends and issues; book and software reviews; columns about taxes and language usage; reports on EFA meetings and activities; and more. In 2009, it became available electronically for those members requesting it, which led to substantial savings in printing and mailing.[12]

The **Publications Committee** is one of the oldest and longest-running committees of the EFA. It existed in 1976 along with the Benefits and Structure Committees, which have since morphed into other committees. The organization's Booklet Campaign has generated a library of 42 titles that are for sale as ebooks, PDF downloads, or paperbacks. These booklets, written by EFA members, cover topics of particular interest to freelancers. The booklets are approximately 5,000 to 14,000 words. The chairperson of this committee, currently Robin Martin, arranges acquisitions, editing, and publishing of the booklets. Some current titles are:

A Freelancer's Guide to Difficult Clients, by Ann Kellett

Google Docs for Editors, by Karin Horler

A Guide for the Freelance Indexer, by April Michelle Davis

Just the Facts: On Researching Your Nonfiction Children's Book, by Lisa L. Owens

Sensitivity Reads, by Ebonye Gussine Wilkins & Lourdes Venard

---

11 Annual Report, 2007
12 Annual Report, 2009

The monthly **ebulletin**, *What's New at the EFA*, continues to exceed the industry open rate standard of 22.6 percent with its average open rate of 31.5 percent. With a new design in 2020 that is more compatible with the EFA brand, this monthly communication tool provides EFA members with up-to-date information on benefits, events, and resources available to them.

Started by Andrew Huston, the inaugural issue was emailed to members on October 9, 2014. The ebulletin was developed not only to keep members informed of EFA's many resources, events, and benefits, but to draw traffic to our website and social media sites, inform members about our courses, and encourage participation in chapter activities and industry events.

In addition to Andrew Huston, EFA is indebted to several others who helped get *What's New* off the ground during its first year, including Susannah Driver-Barstow, Christina M. Frey, Bill Keenan, and Jennifer Maybin.

In 2017, Luann Reed-Siegel became editor of *What's New*, with Lila Stromer serving as proofreader. Denise Larrabee is the current editor, and Lila Stromer continues to volunteer her time as proofreader. In 2019, EFA Events and Communications Coordinator Vina Orden was instrumental in the redesign of the ebulletin. The new design was launched with the January 2020 issue, just in time to begin celebrating EFA's fiftieth anniversary.

In 2020, the EFA has achieved an active presence on the most popular **social media platforms**—EFA members can engage with the organization and other members on Facebook, Twitter, LinkedIn, and Instagram. All are great platforms for keeping up with the EFA's latest news and events and making new connections. They also help us maintain a professional social media presence for the EFA and expand our reach beyond the EFA membership. The administrators of these accounts work closely with the Website committee and Advertising group to help keep EFA's online presence consistent and accessible.

The EFA first ventured into the use of social media in 2010 with Facebook, LinkedIn, and Twitter, and quickly attracted followers on each platform. They have grown considerably over the years, along with EFA members' reliance on them to remain connected to each other. Within three years of its launch, the EFA Facebook page, started by Lisa Owens and now administered by Ruth Mullen, had 5,000 followers, which doubled by 2018. Today it has 13,515 followers. The LinkedIn EFA company page was launched by Susannah Driver-Barstow in 2019 and is now managed by Vina Orden. As of November 2020, it has 13,536 followers. The LinkedIn group page was launched by Ruth E. Thaler-Carter in 2008, and was later picked up by Member at Large (MAL) Bob Faszczewski. Intended to be members only, this group page is onerous and redundant, so will be discontinued in 2020. The Twitter account, started by Erin Wilcox and currently administered by Sarah Cypher and her team of tweeters, reached 5,000 followers in 2016 and has 14,000 followers today.

The Twitter team hosts Freelance Friday, a monthly, one-hour opportunity to meet with other freelancers across the globe in an energetic exchange of questions, answers, and insights into all things freelance. Each month a different topic is the focus. Sometimes a guest specialist on the topic is part of the discussion. And occasionally, they just kick back and enjoy a virtual party. After the hosted portion of the chat, participants can keep discussing tips, pitfalls, the merits of working at home versus renting an office, favorite tools, unsolved problems . . . anything about the freelance life!

In 2019, Tara Kovach added an Instagram account (a must these days!) to EFA's family of social media outlets and, as of today, the EFA has 1,228 followers there. This year, the **Social Media Committee** was formed with Ruth Mullen as its chairperson, making it the EFA's newest committee of record. The Social Media chairperson keeps each team on brand and supports their efforts to engage with EFA members and spread the word about the organization's mission.

Discounts from affiliates are particularly popular with EFA members, and the EFA has been offering such benefits since at least 1995. That year, Cambridge University Press offered EFA members a 20 percent discount on the purchase *of Editing Fact and Fiction* and *Scientific Style and Format*. Another early and popular benefit for EFA members was a subscription to *Vocabula Review*, an online resource on the English language in a blog format.

The chairperson of the **Membership Committee** actively seeks outside affiliate benefits for EFA members. In 2020, these affiliates include

JSTOR, Mutual of Omaha, PEN America, Upflex, SfEP, IngramSpark, Jane Friedman's *The Hot Sheet*, Editors Canada, and *The Copyeditors Workbook and Handbook*, among others. The current chairperson, Michael Coffino, sent a survey to members in August 2020 to get new ideas for affiliate offerings.

Former board member Amy Fass was the longtime chairperson of the now defunct **Healthcare Committee**. She deftly navigated the organization through the changes to the healthcare system under the Obama administration, which was no small task. According to Sheila Buff:

> For decades before ACA, EFA did offer a group health insurance plan through TEIGIT, an umbrella group of NYC-based arts organizations. With some exceptions, the plan could cover only members in the greater NYC area. When we began the program in the 1970s, that wasn't much of an issue because most members lived in the city. The plan was reasonably good and was less expensive than buying one individually, but even so we never had more than about 120 participants. This small group shrank over time and also became a much smaller percentage of the total membership as EFA grew both in numbers and geographic reach. It was also a real administrative burden for the organization even after we brought in a third-party administrator to handle it.

Group plans like TEIGIT were eliminated under ACA. Because EFA is a professional association and not a union, under current law we can't offer group health insurance, but, Buff says, "In general, similar plans can be purchased individually on the ACA exchanges for about the same price or lower, sometimes substantially lower, depending on income."

In 2020, discounted rates on healthcare services, including dental, are available through third-party providers for EFA members in some areas of the United States. The EFA does not provide any health insurance directly. Healthcare discount plans are available to members only. The administrators are very efficient, and new members are generally enrolled quickly. In addition to the plans offered through Careington and DentalSave, EFA members receive discounts on disability, long-term care, and critical illness insurance premiums through Mutual of Omaha.

Beyond classes, booklets, and affiliate deals, the EFA provides benefits to its members that you can't put a price on.

The **Diversity Initiative**, co-founded by EFA Board Members Sangeeta Mehta and Christina M. Frey, has been embraced by the organization as a way to build a more-welcoming and inclusive environment for all of our editorial freelance professionals, including those members who are notably underrepresented in our ranks, and to help make the EFA a multicultural network of ideas, experience, perspectives, and knowledge.

The DI, as it is commonly known, wrote the nondiscrimination statement all members must now acknowledge when they join. They also developed a best-practices guide for how to use inclusive language and in September 2020 launched the Word List of Diversity and Contested Terms, a list of words that often appear in diversity discourse and should be kept in mind during editing. That list is accessible from both the Diversity Initiative page and the Essential Reading section of the Member Area page on the-efa.org.

The Welcome Program launched by the DI in 2019 is a three-month program that pairs established members/freelancers (welcomers) with new members (newcomers) to help them familiarize themselves with the EFA. This involved establishing guidelines for both welcomers and newcomers, creating intake surveys, holding an orientation, and sending out exit surveys. The initial programs were a tremendous success, and the second official session is about to launch as this booklet is being put together.

The DI is working to increase our members' awareness of the publishing industry's history of explicit and implicit bias and of the organization's ongoing efforts to address issues of equity both in our organization and the greater editorial freelance culture.

This year of the organization's fiftieth anniversary may well be remembered as an important year for bringing awareness of ongoing discrimination to the fore. The Black Lives Matter movement forced many organizations and businesses to finally take actions towards diversity, equity, and inclusion. Having these things in an organization are a benefit for all members. We have, in part, the influence of our DI leaders to thank for making this a priority in 2020.

In addition to providing the affiliate benefits mentioned earlier, the **Membership Committee** is at the heart of EFA's efforts to create and sustain our community. This committee's chairperson looks for members to feature in an occasional "spotlight," published on the website to coincide with the publication of the *Freelancer*. The Member Spotlight was introduced in September 2012 by Cassie Tuttle, the Membership chairperson at the time. She also developed the survey to collect information about why people let their membership lapse, which we began sending out in 2014.

The Membership Committee makes the effort to survey members in order for the organization to better serve them. In 1991 they created the first common-rates survey. In 2019, the PR group took over management of the survey (see below).

The **Public Relations (PR)** (led by Sangeeta Mehta) and **Advertising** (led by Sheila Buff) groups are ad-hoc committees created in the spring of 2016 to provide benefits for our members on three primary fronts:

1. Bringing potential clients to the Job List and the Member Directory.
2. Building the reputation and visibility of the organization to increase the value of membership.
3. Increasing the size of the member community and knowledge base.

In 2016, the EFA Board of Governors approved the selection of an ad agency to create the first-ever sustained ad campaign and the resources to fund it. Sheila Buff has been working with Robot House to create and sustain advertising campaigns that began with coming up with clever taglines, such as the current: "The Right Editor. Right Away." They also came up with the all-important (at the time) Google Ad-words campaigns, like: *Another Set of Eyes Never Hurt – Just Ask the Cyclops findtherighteditor.com The right skills. The right reputation. The right results. Right away.* And, *If Hemingway Had Our Editors – He'd Write Drunk, Edit Never findtherighteditor.com Because mistakes are as embarrassing as dangling your participle in public.* Robot House, Sheila, and Susannah Driver-Barstow worked together to select the models for two different advertising photo shoots set up by Robot House for our advertising and branding.

The PR group has written numerous press releases about events and conferences where the EFA has exhibited. They have also run several social media campaigns, ranging from a grammar-tips series to quotations by famous authors, to an extensive and ongoing "Meet the EFA Instructor" campaign, conceived by volunteer Lauren Duensing, which promotes the EFA's diverse educational offerings.

Since 2017, the PR group has also sent follow-up notes to those who have provided their contact information at events; promoted raffles, which give participants the chance to win EFA swag and have gone a long way in helping the EFA build our email list. In 2018, they also created a photo library to share with various EFA committees, including the social media, newsletter, and website teams.

According to Sangeeta Mehta, one of the proudest achievements of this committee was creating a promotional video in 2017 that featured EFA members. "We hired a videographer to film volunteers at the Writer's Digest Conference and sorted through hours of footage to come up with this one-minute segment about what membership means to us." The following year, they created a second video, which features the co-executives and staff of the EFA and explains how the EFA's Job List works.

One might suppose that the predecessor of the **Website Committee** was the Computer Committee, as indicated by this piece of EFA newsletter content in 1984 announcing an exciting new development for the organization:

> EFA is operational in a new key! During the summer, EFA's Computer Committee keyed in E-N-D to its search-and-choose procedures for a standalone, high-quality, medium-priced microcomputer with word-processing and record keeping (alphabetic, numeric) capabilities. The microcomputer selected . . . is a DEC Rainbow 100 (dual-disk drive), with software customized to our needs: Multi-Plan, WordStar 3.30, dBase II.[13]

The EFA launched a new website in October 1997. The website included benefits information, publications, links to resources, and membership information. At the time, it was receiving 350 visits per

---

13 May/June 1984 *News!*

week, and it was hoped it would generate more members beyond the New York metropolitan area.

By 2007, it was determined that the website needed a "facelift," which was conducted under the leadership of Helen Glenn Court, chairperson at the time. This increased traffic to the site, which more than doubled over 2006 numbers and then quadrupled in 2008.[14] Also that year, a Members area was added, and the Member Directory database was integrated with the website, allowing members to maintain their own records and directory listings.

In 2012, under the leadership of Karen Wallace, several pages were added: a Member Spotlight page, Job List and membership testimonial pages, and a page for uploading Twitter transcripts. A New Members page followed in 2014. The most visited pages at the time were those containing membership information and resources, public resources, editorial rates, regional chapters, the Member Directory, the Job List, news, and the education catalog.

Working with the website design team, database function, and all backend issues of the-efa.org, the Website Committee chairperson is the one who hears about any website malfunction and has to find the solution. The Website chairperson is the point person for any decisions regarding a website redesign: the latest began in 2014 and took nearly three years to complete.

The new design, launched in 2017, took into account suggestions from members in email messages and on a membership survey. Improvements included a modern design and intuitive navigation; separate sections for members, prospective members and clients; a more powerful directory search; revised and expanded specialties, skills, and materials options; online renewal during the grace period and rejoining after the grace period; and expanded events and news for the organization and for chapters. Much attention went into making the site attractive, uncluttered, and easy to navigate.

In January through September of our fiftieth year, members and guests completed the following transactions through the EFA website:

---

14 Annual Reports, 2007, 2008

50 Years of the EFA

- joins and renewals: 1,974
- guest signups: 1,966
- course and webinar registrations: 3,405

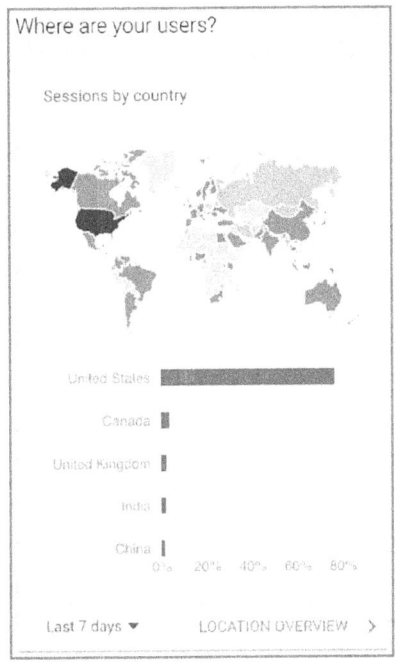

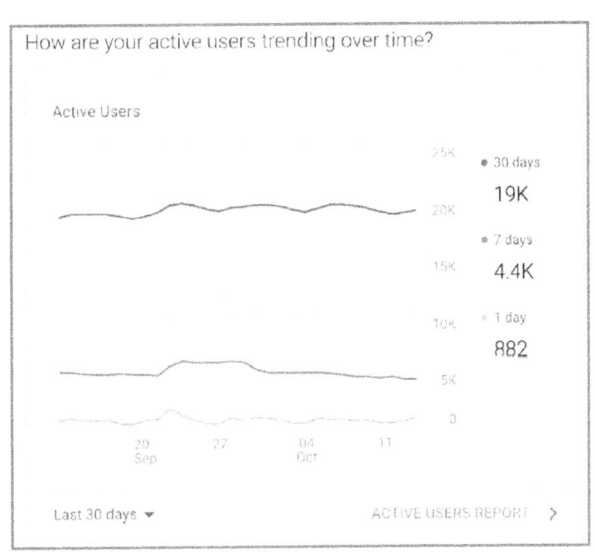

Other, perhaps unsung, benefits to members of the EFA include the **vast resources for potential clients**. We educate them so you don't have to!

By far our most popular resource in this area is our rates chart. The **rates survey** provides a tabulation of members' rates for various types of writing and editing work as reported in a confidential poll of the membership. The PR group conducted the rates survey of the membership in 2020, after an arduous years-long preparation process. They received 578 returned surveys. A total of 2,742 EFA members successfully received the survey, making the return rate at about 21 percent.

According to consultant Angela Darchi, "This is a very good response! Most email surveys generate less than 10 percent."

The results of the rates survey are posted on the EFA website, one of the most visited pages at the-efa.org and widely used as a reference point by members, clients, and other freelancers.

In addition to the rates chart, potential clients are educated about editing tests and sample edits, given guidance on how to Find a Freelancer and use our Member Directory and Job List, are introduced to the different types of editing and how to hire an editor, and what to expect from the freelancer-client relationship. Our **Guide for New Authors** and self-publishers provides support and answers to commonly asked questions.

Being able to direct a potential client to these resources is a tremendous benefit!

Certainly, our editorial freelance community has benefitted and will continue to benefit from all of these member-driven initiatives and achievements, and at this fifty-year commemoration, we are just ramping up! The growth and development of the organization, its members, and its engagement with the outside world is at an exciting point. This look back at the way the EFA has come to be the dynamic organization it is today in 2020 reveals an impressive history. It's important to reflect, though, on the fact that this organization is much like a large trans-oceanic freighter. It is stable and focused, and it takes a tremendous amount of power, planning, and patience to make any changes in our trajectory. But changes do happen—our members working together make them happen—and the freighter advances wave over wave.

Thank you to the founders, builders, all of the board members, and countless other volunteers, for the time, energy, and effort you have put into growing this organization over the past fifty years.

About the Editorial Freelancers Association (EFA)

Celebrating 50 Years!
Dedicated to the Education and Growth
of Editorial Freelancers

The EFA is a national not-for-profit — 501(c)6 — organization, headquartered in New York City, run by member volunteers, all of whom are also freelancers. The EFA's members, experienced in a wide range of professional skills, live and work all across the United States and in other countries.

A pioneer in organizing freelancers into a network for mutual support and advancement, the EFA is now recognized throughout the publishing industry as the source for professional editorial assistance.

We welcome people of every race, color, culture, religion or no religion, gender identity, gender expression, age, national or ethnic origin, ancestry, citizenship, education, ability, health, neurotype, marital/parental status, socio-economic background, sexual orientation, and/or military status. We are nothing without our members, and encourage everyone to volunteer and to participate in our community.

The EFA sells a variety of specialized booklets, not unlike this one, on topics of interest to editorial freelancers at the-efa.org.

The EFA hosts online, asynchronous courses, real-time webinars, and on-demand recorded webinars designed especially for freelance editors, writers, and other editorial specialists around the world. You can learn more about our Education Program at the-efa.org.

To learn about these and other EFA offerings, visit the-efa.org and join us on social media:

Twitter: @EFAFreelancers
Instagram: @efa_editors
Facebook: editorialfreelancersassociation
LinkedIn: editorial-freelancers

www.ingramcontent.com/pod-product-compliance
Lightning Source LLC
Chambersburg PA
CBHW071544080526
44588CB00011B/1781